CONVERSATIONS WITH
OSCAR WILDE

Merlin Holland is the only grandson of Oscar Wilde. For the last thirty years he has been researching his grandfather's life and works. He is the co-editor of *The Complete Letters of Oscar Wilde* and author of *The Wilde Album* and *Irish Peacock and Scarlet Marquess*, the first uncensored publication of his 1895 libel trial.

Simon Callow is a film, TV and theatre actor, as well as a writer. He played Oscar Wilde on stage in *The Importance of Being Oscar*, and his books include *Oscar Wilde and His Circle*.

Learn about key figures in science, spirituality, art and literature through revealing dialogues based on established fact. Written by a fantastic collection of authors and foreword writers gathered together to delve into the lives and achievements of some of the world's greatest historical figures, this series is perfect for anyone looking for a quick and accessible introduction to the subject.

OTHER TITLES IN THE SERIES

Published

Conversations with JFK
by Michael O'Brien; Foreword by Gore Vidal

Conversations with Casanova
by Derek Parker; Foreword by Dita Von Teese

Forthcoming

Conversations with Buddha
by Joan Duncan Oliver; Foreword by Annie Lennox

Conversations with Dickens
by Paul Schlicke; Foreword by Peter Ackroyd

Conversations with Galileo
by William Shea; Foreword by Dava Sobel

For Rupert,
who also recreated Oscar in Paris,
with love.

CONVERSATIONS WITH OSCAR WILDE

A FICTIONAL DIALOGUE BASED
ON BIOGRAPHICAL FACTS

Merlin Holland

Foreword by Simon Callow

WATKINS
Sharing Wisdom Since 1893

Originally published under the title *Coffee with Oscar Wilde* 2007
This edition first published in the UK and USA 2019 by
Watkins, an imprint of Watkins Media Limited

Unit 11, Shepperton House
89–93 Shepperton Road
London
N1 3DF
enquiries@watkinspublishing.com

Design and typography copyright © Watkins Media Limited 2019

Text copyright © Merlin Holland 2007, 2019
Foreword copyright © Simon Callow 2007, 2019

10 9 8 7 6 5 4 3 2 1

Typeset by JCS Publishing Services Ltd

Printed and bound by TJ International Ltd, Padstow, Cornwall

A CIP record for this book is available from the British Library

ISBN: 978-1-78678-230-4

www.watkinspublishing.com

CONTENTS

Foreword by Simon Callow   ix
Introduction   1
Oscar Wilde (1854–1900): His Life in Short   5

Now Let's Start Talking ...
Introducing Mr Wilde   19
Student of Greek   25
Professor of Aesthetics   31
Discovering America   37
Almost Respectable   43
Shocking the Middle Classes   49
Feasting with Panthers   55
A Fatal Friendship   61
The Libel Trial   69
Decadence Discredited   79
The Artist in Prison   85
A Sort of Freedom   93
The Last Act   99
After Oscar   107

Further Reading   115

FOREWORD BY SIMON CALLOW

Oscar Wilde's fame has never been greater. He is celebrated as dramatist, novelist, essayist, poet, gay martyr. His savage treatment at the hands of the English law was for many generations a potent image of its vicious absurdity, and its eventual reform is in some senses a posthumous redemption of his suffering.

But over and above admiration for his literary achievements and pity for his cruel destiny, it is above all affection that Oscar Wilde inspires. He regularly tops those lists, compiled from time to time, of ideal dinner guests, past or present. His charm has persisted in a way that is true of very few of the great charmers of the past. Is there a more delightful volume in the English language than his *Complete Letters* (despite the sombre presence among them of *De Profundis*, which he wrote in prison)? We have no physical record of the fabled beauty of his speaking voice, alas, but the quite substantial fragments of his conversation written down by his contemporaries still make one beam with pleasure, even laugh out loud.

Wilde was not a selfish speaker. He really listened and responded, and was as free with his own laughter as he was skilled at provoking it in others (though, disarmingly, he was unable to resist laughing at his own jokes). His principal comic method was inversion, standing cliché on its head, spinning surreal fantasies which often left his audience literally helpless with laughter. The effect was tonic, and it is entirely possible to believe his early biographer and friend Robert Sherard when he writes that Wilde had arrived one day at his house to be greeted by Sherard's ashen-faced maid, under instructions to turn away all visitors on account of her master's violent toothache. Wilde persisted, and finding Sherard moaning, prostrate, in a darkened room, embarked on an account of his day so fascinating and so droll that little by little Sherard's pain disappeared, not to return.

Wilde's personality was undoubtedly a performance, but it was a generous one, and not without cost to himself. One night, it is reported, having left his hat behind, he returned to a party which minutes earlier he had held enraptured with his apparently effortless wit and bonhomie, and his host was shocked to find him drained, almost spent, unable to put two coherent words together. Prison temporarily dimmed his ability to joke, but despite persistent physical and financial misery, his wit after his release was if anything even more fantastical and prodigal than before. His incomparable deathbed observations about the wallpaper ("one of us had to go") have become almost proverbial; but it is another utterance from his dying days, almost his last words, addressed to that most loyal of friends, Robert Ross, that perfectly catches his sublime naughtiness: "Dear Robbie, when the Last Trumpet sounds and we are couched in our porphyry tombs, I shall turn and whisper to you, 'Robbie, dear Robbie, let us pretend we do not hear it.'"

INTRODUCTION

A meeting with Oscar Wilde over several cups
of coffee one rainy afternoon in Paris has been a
delight. But to conjure this has been a challenge,
too, as attempting to recreate his conversational
style for this book has required almost the same
level of hubris as Oscar Wilde himself taking
on the Marquess of Queensberry for libel back
in 1895, and hoping he could get away with
it simply because of who he was. How could
anyone presume to put words into the mouth of
one of the greatest conversationalists of all time
and not risk the wrath of Nemesis? The cowardly
solution would have been to cut out the best
quotations from his works and letters and sew
them back together in some sort of coherent
form, so that no one could accuse me of trying
to out-Oscar Oscar. The result, I fear, would have
been one of those books of indigestible Wilde
one-liners taken out of context, with a good
many of the seams showing. This would have
irritated readers at all familiar with his works

who couldn't remember where the quotes had come from, and anyway would have wondered what they were doing here.

By way of compromise I have adopted a different principle, which has been to boil all the ingredients up together so that they still have the flavour of Oscar Wilde without always being instantly recognizable. In some cases this has meant taking quotations and changing the person, the tense or the mood so that what he originally expressed in writing becomes as near as possible to direct speech without losing his style. In other cases I have amalgamated quotes or otherwise reduced them, inverted them or used them in a context for which they were not originally intended. While this is no justification, at least we have a Wildean precedent for such a practice. Not long after finishing *The Picture of Dorian Gray*, Oscar started work on *Lady Windermere's Fan* and, never one to waste a good epigram, gave new life to many of those used in the novel by weaving them into the play. In order to avoid neologisms wherever possible but still enable the dialogue to flow, I checked Wilde's phraseology by doing word searches on digitized texts. This revealed, not unexpectedly, just how modern his language was for the 1890s.

I considered at length whether to adopt a thematic or a biographical approach to Oscar and concluded that since his work and his life were so inextricably linked, he would be more likely to confide in us about both when speaking about himself. That said, when he is talking about the first part of his life, in which he wore a multiplicity of disguises, we can never be quite sure whether to take his remarks at face value; by contrast, when he reflects on the last part, in which he was stripped even of his dignity, all he has left is his humour to protect him, and that greatest of gifts, the ability to smile at his own misfortune. As he said, "Pain, unlike Pleasure, wears no mask." I was also mindful of a story told to me by the late Sheridan Morley, the theatre critic. One day he received a letter from the publisher George Weidenfeld asking him to write a biography of Wilde. Sheridan rang him up and asked why – there had been one published only ten years before. "Yes," said Weidenfeld, "but it's such a good story that the public needs to be retold it every decade or so." In this opinion, Mr Wilde himself seems entirely to concur.

OSCAR WILDE (1854–1900)
HIS LIFE IN SHORT

The life of Oscar Wilde has all the elements of
a firework display: first the excited anticipation,
then the spectacular show, a near-deafening
explosion for the climax, and finally – silence. In
an uncanny way he anticipated it all in his story
of "The Remarkable Rocket" which, rising as if
from nowhere in a shower of sparks, explodes
and falls to earth, exclaiming as it goes out,
"I knew I should create a great sensation."

He was born at 21 Westland Row, Dublin, on
16 October 1854 and christened Oscar Fingal
O'Flahertie Wills Wilde. He was embarrassed
by this mouthful of names at school, proud at
university, and dismissive of them in later life,
saying, "As one becomes famous, one sheds
some of them, just as a balloonist, when rising
higher, sheds unnecessary ballast. All but two

have already been thrown overboard. Soon I shall discard another and be known simply as 'The Wilde' or 'The Oscar'." Over a century later, as with much else that he said, this apparently incredible claim has proved to be unnervingly accurate.

As the younger son of William and Jane Francesca (or Speranza, as she liked, poetically, to style herself), he grew up in what today would be regarded as comfortable, upper-middle-class, professional surroundings. The family moved to Merrion Square shortly after Oscar was born, to an ample Georgian house where William Wilde practised as one of the foremost ear and eye surgeons of his day. Apart from his medical eminence, he was also a recognized authority on the folklore, natural history, ethnology and topography of Ireland, wrote on Dean Swift and was knighted in 1864 for his pioneering work with the Irish censuses since 1841 – a true Victorian polymath. His mother, a committed Nationalist, had written inflammatory poems for the *Nation* newspaper at the time of the Irish famine and had narrowly avoided imprisonment. She was a gifted linguist (she translated from the French and German), shared her husband's love of all things Irish and ran one of Dublin's most stimulating literary salons. Such was Oscar Wilde's heritage. The child was weaned on words.

His early life in Ireland was marked by two events — a scandal and a tragedy. In 1864, his parents became embroiled in a very public libel case with overtones of sexual misconduct, brought by one of Sir William's former patients; and in 1867 Oscar's younger sister, Isola, to whom he was deeply attached, died of a fever. On a happier note, he won most of the Classics prizes and scholarships which were on offer at school and university. He wasted time constructively like any modern undergraduate, first at Trinity College, Dublin, and then at Magdalen College, Oxford. At Oxford he was awarded a degree described as the finest of his year, after which he arrived in London ready, as he said, to set the world on fire. While at Oxford he had befriended John Ruskin and Walter Pater, and had attached himself conspicuously to the new and controversial "Aesthetic Movement" in art and poetry. This was largely a pose to get himself noticed, as he had published very little by then apart from a few poems and a review of the new Grosvenor Gallery, but it was a pose he continued in order to further his campaign of self-publicity. Once in London he wrote his first play, *Vera* – a melodrama about Russian anarchists – in 1880, but failed to get it staged, partly for political reasons. The following year he published a volume of poetry in a modest print-run of 750, dividing it artificially into first, second and third editions in order to exaggerate its success. Despite selling out, the volume had a mixed critical reception, and Oscar's ego was further bruised by the Oxford Union Library first soliciting a copy and then returning it as unwanted.

At the end of 1881, Oscar was invited to make a lecture tour of the United States as a showpiece "aesthete", so that the American public could more easily understand the satire of the new Gilbert and Sullivan operetta *Patience*. It was, however, no foppish young dandy – as the aesthetes were commonly portrayed – who could deliver 140 lectures in 260 days, drink the members of San Francisco's Bohemian Club under the table and match the whiskey-drinking miners of Leadville, Colorado, glass for glass. He stayed in the States for a year, achieved something halfway between fame and notoriety, and returned with the modern equivalent of about £100,000 ($130,000) in his pocket.

Literary laurels, however, still eluded him. For four years after his return from America he found himself obliged to make a living as a book reviewer, occasional theatre critic and lecturer on, among other things, interior decoration and dress. In the meantime, in 1884, he married Constance Lloyd, who gave him two children in quick succession – Cyril in 1885 and Vyvyan in 1886.

Then, in the spring of 1887, Cassell & Co. approached Oscar to help them relaunch an ailing magazine, *The Lady's World*. He accepted the challenge but insisted that it be renamed *Woman's World*, saying: "At present it is too feminine and not sufficiently womanly ... we should deal not merely with what women wear but with what they think, and what they feel." He changed the magazine's name in support of the proto-feminist New Woman movement which was attracting increasing attention, not all of it positive. His time as editor of *Woman's World* is sometimes regarded by his biographers as an interesting but unimportant interlude in his writing life. It was more than that: it established him as a front-line writer; it relieved the acute financial pressures of family life; and above all it gave him time for pure literary work. *Woman's*

World effectively kick-started the great creative
period of his life, as well as giving us a rare
glimpse of a socially conscious Oscar Wilde.

Over the next eight years Oscar produced
almost all his best work. The range was
remarkable: short stories (*The Happy Prince and
Other Tales*, 1888); essays, dialogues and literary
criticism; a novel (*The Picture of Dorian Gray*,
1891); prose poems and poetry (*The Sphinx*,
1894); and all his major plays (*Lady Windermere's
Fan*, 1892; *A Woman of No Importance*, 1893;
and *An Ideal Husband* and *The Importance of
Being Earnest*, both in 1895). However, a subtle
change takes place in the moral standpoint of his
fiction between 1887 and 1895, which seems
to provide a dark reflection of the upheavals in
his own life. From the redemptive qualities that
allow young Virginia to lay Sir Simon's soul to
rest in *The Canterville Ghost* (1887) and the
deeply Christian, almost parable-like "The Selfish
Giant" and "The Happy Prince" (1888), he
progresses through the cynical "The Nightingale
and the Rose" (1888) to the dark and disturbing
conclusions of *The Picture of Dorian Gray* (1891)
and "The Fisherman and His Soul" (1891), in
both of which the concept of beauty has become

associated with temptation, danger and death. The change in tone reaches a climax with his play *Salomé*, which was banned from the London stage in 1892 while Sarah Bernhardt was in rehearsal (the ban was not officially lifted until the 1930s). This was a tormented period for Wilde during which, still married, he became aware of his homosexuality and the need at that stage to hide it not only from his family but from society at large (male homosexual acts were criminalized in English law in 1885). Under the veneer of glittering epigrams in his Society plays run the disturbing themes of abandonment, illegitimacy, concealment and double lives.

In 1891 Oscar Wilde fell in love with a young aristocrat, Alfred Douglas, the third son of the Marquess of Queensberry. With that love came tragedy, financial ruin and disgrace. By the beginning of 1895, no longer merely a publicity-seeking aethete but a mature, successful dramatist, Oscar had two plays running simultaneously in London's West End, bringing in the modern equivalent of £7,000 ($9,000) a week. London Society could not make up its mind whether it found him fascinating or horrifying – whether to court him for his charm or cut him for his morals. Then, in April 1895, Wilde sued Queensberry for criminal libel after the Marquess had left an insulting card at Wilde's club. The action collapsed after the defence exposed Wilde's private life in court, and he was arrested the same evening on charges of "gross indecency". His fall was nothing short of spectacular. His plays continued to run, with the author's name pasted out on the billboards; then they were taken off. His books were removed from sale. His works were effectively suppressed and almost overnight he became penniless. Within three weeks his creditors had sent in the bailiffs to auction the contents of his Chelsea house in Tite Street; within a month his two children had been forced to leave the country. By the end of May he had been tried for homosexual acts and convicted. He served two years in prison. Released in 1897, he lived his last years in exile, mainly in France, under the assumed name Sebastian Melmoth. He died of meningitis in Paris on 30 November 1900 at the age of 46.

———

While he was alive, Oscar Wilde lived in fear, as he said, of his public *not* misunderstanding him. "Be warned in time, and remain, as I do, incomprehensible," he wrote to the painter James Whistler in 1885. "To be great is to be misunderstood", and he spent the rest of his life trying to ensure that he was. Myths, masks and mystery had been his stock-in-trade from early on. "What is true about a man's life is not what he does, but the legend which he creates around himself," he said to a French reporter, Jacques Daurelle, in 1891. "You must never destroy legends; it is through them we are given a glimpse of the real face of a man." And as if to emphasize the point, he added: "I have never walked the streets of London with a lily in my hand, for any caretaker or coachman could have done the same. No, to have done it would have been nothing; but to make people *believe* that I had done it – that was a triumph."

Now, over 100 years after his death, Oscar Wilde still manages to be enigmatic – the ultimate tribute to the prince of the art of paradox. We are fascinated by the duality of the man, confused by the apparent contradictions both in his life and in his work, but forced to wonder how many of them were contrived for effect and how many are simply part of the inherent richness of his complicated, multifaceted character. What are we to make of this Anglo-Irishman with Nationalist sympathies who supported Home Rule for Ireland; this Protestant with life-long Catholic leanings; this married homosexual with two children; this musician of words and painter of language, who confessed to André Gide that writing bored him; this artist astride not two but three cultures – an Anglo-Francophile who was a Celt at heart; this conformist rebel who toed Society's line for just long enough that it would laugh when he put his thumb to his nose? Perhaps the answer is that what we see as contradictions on the surface are in fact different but complementary aspects of the same reality, and that the ever-shifting interplay between them is the kaleidoscopic nature of Oscar Wilde. Try to pin him down, dissect him and label the parts logically, and the spirit of the man is lost. He himself understood this perfectly. As he wrote at the end of his essay "The Truth of Masks": "In art there is no such thing as a universal truth. A Truth in art is that whose contradictory is also true."

His relentless self-promotion during his life as a dandy, wit, conversationalist and writer of comedies ensured for decades after his death that any reputation he may have had as a scholar and a thinker was put firmly aside. Instead, he was regarded as something of a first-rate funny-man struggling to rise beyond the second division of literary excellence. Of course, it is tempting to think that this is just as he would have wished it to be – the life taking precedence over the works, the genius, as he saw it, over the talent. But like all things to do with Wilde, the obvious is not the reality but the mask that hides it.

Was he simply a passing socio-cultural phenomenon and the author of lightweight popular works? Or was he a thoroughly modern thinker, bridging two centuries, an astute critic and commentator, a writer at odds with the stuffiness of his age, whose "over-the-topness in knocking the bottom out of things," in Seamus Heaney's words, amused but finally enraged his tight-laced Victorian contemporaries? However much the critical view of Wilde and his work may change, he seems to be assured of a permanent place in the heart of his public. There has always been a sneaking admiration not only for a rebel who pushes life to the limits and then has the courage to stand by what he has done, but especially for a man whose wit and humour can still bring such pleasure to so many.

NOW LET'S START TALKING ...

Over the following pages, Oscar Wilde engages in an imaginary conversation covering 14 themes, responding freely to searching questions.

The questions are in bold type;
Wilde's answers are in normal type.

INTRODUCING
MR WILDE

Paris was something of a spiritual home to Oscar Wilde. He once said, "It is the most wonderful city in the world, the only civilized capital; the only place on earth where you find absolute tolerance for all human frailties." He spoke French fluently and spent up to three months in Paris on several occasions, meeting Victor Hugo, Paul Verlaine and André Gide. It was there that he wrote much of his controversial play *Salomé*, in 1891, and when it was banned in England he even threatened to take French nationality. There seemed no more appropriate place in which to ask him about his life and work.

Well, dear boy, this is a surprise, but a very pleasant one, and I'm delighted that you decided on Paris. I don't think I could have faced going back to London, even after all this time. Beer, the Bible and the Seven Deadly Virtues made the English what they were in my time – anti-artistic and narrow-minded – and I don't imagine there's been much change since I left back in 1897. When I say left, I didn't exactly leave, you know. They sent me to prison for two years, which was as good as being sent into exile, and the day I was released I came over to France. Such a civilized country, I always think, where the artist is respected and nobody cares much what goes on behind closed doors – and I adore the language. To me there are only two languages in the world: French and Greek. In fact, I once wrote a play in French ... but here we are, hardly through the door and barely acquainted and I'm addressing you with all the tediousness of an old friend. Where shall we sit? Somewhere I can enjoy a cigarette. You don't mind if I smoke, do you?

Well, no, but I'm afraid that it's no longer the sophisticated pastime that it was in your day.

Even in Paris, there are laws now about where one can and one can't, and …

How tiresome. I always maintain that a cigarette is the perfect type of a perfect pleasure: it is exquisite, and it leaves one unsatisfied. So I suppose that smoking, except between consenting adults in private, is in danger of becoming a criminal offence. Now, since we have paid our lip service to modernity and started with the end, let us be thoroughly avant-garde and go back to the beginning.

Actually, that's just what I was going to suggest, especially as you once told André Gide that you had put your genius into your life but only your talent into your works. It seems to me that you've always seen your life as a work of art.

Exactly – and I understood that very early on, even if I wasn't aware of the implications it would have. In life, style, not sincerity, is the essential – that was a lesson my mother taught me. Not that she wasn't sincere when it came to her feelings about Ireland and the English, but style was her hallmark – style tinged with a love of the unusual, the exotic, the bizarre. Oh, she loved being "Lady Wilde", wife of the internationally respected Sir William, but as a student I always remember the time a friend of the family asked if she could bring a "respectable" acquaintance to one of our Saturday soirées. "Respectable!" exclaimed my mother. "Never use that word here. Only tradesmen are respectable." And from then on I used to invite friends home to meet Mama saying that she and I had founded a Society for the Suppression of Virtue.

This fascination with wickedness, the rejection of all those proper middle-class values the Victorians were so keen on — that's something with which you're always associated. Doesn't that make you feel a little uncomfortable?

Certainly not. Wickedness is simply a myth invented by the good and the respectable to account for the curious attractiveness of others. Good people exasperate one's reason; bad people stir one's imagination. That's why criminals have always fascinated me, and it undoubtedly got me into trouble later on. But just because one chooses to write about people whose behaviour the critics brand as immoral doesn't mean to say that one necessarily subscribes to that view oneself. It's a very involved subject, art and morality, and one which I'd rather go into later when you understand how I came to publish some of the things that I did.

All right. Let's talk a bit more about those formative years. You and your brother Willie had a pretty conventional upbringing really, didn't you?

Yes, in the sense that we were part of Dublin Society, went off to boarding school, studied the classics and took holidays at our country house in County Galway — yes, I suppose so. But that didn't stop me feeling somehow different from my contemporaries. I had a sense of otherness, of a destiny waiting to be fulfilled. I even said one day that I'd like nothing better in later life than to go down in posterity as the defendant in a court case, *Regina* versus *Wilde*. It was a clever but thoroughly unfortunate remark which came back to haunt me 25 years later, when I realized that there are only two tragedies in this world —

one is not getting what one wants and the other is getting it. The second is much the worse. If school taught me anything, it was that not the slightest thing worth knowing can be taught there. For example, my love of Greek and Latin literature, which stayed with me all my life, was as much sensual as intellectual. It would have been a shocking admission to make to a schoolmaster, but I took far more pleasure in handling the classics in beautiful editions and reading aloud, in awakening the strange cadences of those sleeping languages, than I did in the mere translation of the words.

STUDENT OF GREEK

Once he had left Portora, a boarding school in Enniskillen, County Fermanagh, with a scholarship to Trinity College, Dublin, Oscar's whole world began to open up. He crossed the divide between the teacher and the taught and entered the realm where ideas were discussed rather than spoon-fed. It was at Trinity in 1871 that he met John Pentland Mahaffy, who two years before, at the early age of 30, had been appointed Professor of Ancient History.

Apart from your father and mother who, to oversimplify slightly, gave you a lifelong respect for folklore, superstitions and social justice, John Mahaffy was probably the most important influence on you as a young man, wasn't he?

If you don't count John Ruskin and Walter Pater, about whom I'll tell you in a minute, yes. Mahaffy was an extraordinary all-round character – a brilliant intellect, and urbane with it. He was a connoisseur of claret and antiques, fluent in French, German and Italian, and seemed to know half of Europe's royalty. Most important of all, he was a remarkable conversationalist. He seemed to take to me because I had an aptitude for Greek prose which he thought worth fostering, and that was just the beginning. My mind was an empty vessel waiting to be filled, and who better to fill it than he? I preserved the greatest affection and admiration for him for years afterwards. I owed him so much personally – he was my first and my best teacher, the scholar who showed me how to love Greek things, the man who taught me the power of words to charm, to hypnotize, to open every door in any society. I fancy it

was he who said to me that we Irish are too
poetical to be poets — we're a nation of brilliant
failures, but we're the greatest talkers since the
Greeks — and I appropriated his words later as
my own. But why not? Using the oral tradition
as common property was part of the creative
Celtic spirit.

**Despite your academic success at Trinity, after
three years you left without a degree.**

I did — because wider horizons beckoned. I
won myself a scholarship to Magdalen College,
Oxford, partly at Mahaffy's instigation, it must
be said. I think he was proud of the achievement
and sad to lose me, and he managed, as always,
to have the last word: "Better run over to Oxford,
Oscar. You're not quite clever enough for us
here." Even then we didn't lose touch. In the next
three years I travelled twice with him through
Italy and Greece. The second time I wanted to
combine the trip to Greece with a visit to the
Vatican, as the idea of becoming a Catholic was
increasingly attractive to me. Thanks to my old
tutor, though, the potential papist yielded to the
practising pagan. But I arrived back too late for

the spring term and was rusticated by the college. Imagine: I was sent down from Oxford for being the first undergraduate to visit Olympia. Of course, no one in Dublin believed my story and all assumed there was some hidden scandal. It wasn't the last time I got into trouble for telling the truth.

Oxford was a very different place from Trinity, though, wasn't it?

Well, apart from anything else, it was full of the English. I quickly discovered that we had little in common except language, and that only occasionally. If one could only teach the English how to speak and the Irish how to listen, places like Oxford would be quite civilized. English conversation turned out to be rich in evasion and lit by brilliant flashes of silence, not at all what I'd been used to in Dublin. Anyway, one of the first things I did as a compromise was to lose my Irish accent.

Mahaffy may have provided me with some well-honed social skills, but I needed more of a firm intellectual foundation from which to use them. Enter John Ruskin and Walter Pater.

Neither of them really had much to do with my degree course, which was in Classics, because their subject was art criticism and aesthetics. I came to know Ruskin quite well, and some of my dearest memories of Oxford are of my walks and talks with him. His intellectual, noble and high-minded approach to art appealed to one side of me. But there was another side which was fascinated by the decadent, the sensual and the mystical, and that was satisfied by Pater. I read his *Studies in the History of the Renaissance* as soon as I got to Oxford, and it had a strange influence over most of my life.

Not unlike the "poisonous and perfect" book which Lord Henry gives to Dorian Gray?

Exactly. The idea of getting as many pulsations as possible into one's life, to burn always with a hard gem-like flame and to love art for its own sake, was both delightful and dangerous. I remember saying to one of my friends – as we were strolling around Magdalen's narrow bird-haunted walks one morning – that I wanted to eat of the fruit of all the trees in the garden of the world, and that I was going out into the world with that passion in my soul. And that, precisely that, is what I did. I had no intention of becoming a dried-up Oxford don. I was going to be a poet, a writer, a dramatist. Somehow or other I was going to be famous, and if not famous, notorious. In the meantime, I outraged Oxford by declaring that I found it harder every day to live up to my collection of blue-and-white china.

PROFESSOR OF AESTHETICS

Having cultivated an image of idleness and nonchalance, Oscar left Oxford with a double First in Classics and the prestigious Newdigate prize for poetry. The euphoria of success soon wore off, however. He had a small amount of capital on which to set himself up in London, but he urgently needed to find some form of gainful employment. He suggested translating Herodotus to a publisher, applied for an archaeological studentship at Athens, and (not for the last time) put himself forward as an Inspector of Schools. These proposals all came to nothing, so he started networking his way around the capital.

In quite uncharacteristic fashion you started your London life wanting to do various totally conventional jobs. Why?

I suspect that you've only discovered that by reading my letters, which, if I may say so, is both unfair and not very gentlemanly. If you must know, there was a certain amount of family pressure put on me. My father had died a couple of years before, and we discovered that the house in Dublin was mortgaged from cellar to roof, so Willie and I were faced with the prospect of having to support mother. Fortunately, it didn't come to that, though I used to pay her bills whenever I could. Anyway, I soon gave up the idea. I watched young men with bright prospects and perfect profiles come to London and end up complete wrecks in a few months by adopting some useful profession. In an entirely calculated fashion I decided to make a reputation for myself before I'd done anything at all. I was going to become famous for being famous. In that way, as soon as I did achieve something, the public would acknowledge me at once. I took a house with a friend, Frank Miles, who painted Society beauties. I dressed myself

in velvet suits with flowing neckties, grew my
hair and styled myself "Professor of Aesthetics"
and art critic. Frank introduced me to Lily
Langtry who, as it happened, was the mistress
of the Prince of Wales. In no time I'd talked my
way into some of the best houses in London.

Yes, but none of this was making any money.

No, but I was becoming an interesting
phenomenon. I was doing things in ways no one
had thought of doing them before – I turned
convention on its head at a time when convention
was a virtue, and that was fascinating. Even the
Prince of Wales was heard to remark, "I do not
know Mr Wilde and not to know Mr Wilde is
not to be known", so Lily was asked to make
the introduction. I was occasionally accused of
insincerity, but is insincerity such a terrible thing?
I don't think so. It's merely a way in which we can
multiply our personalities. None the less, I was
acutely aware that the novelty of such behaviour
would wear off – Society is notoriously fickle in
its affections – so I started to publish sonnets
to famous actresses about the roles they were
playing. Bernhardt in *Phèdre* was astounding and

my sonnet a remarkable piece of publicity for both of us, coming as it did two weeks after I'd welcomed *la divine Sarah* off the cross-Channel boat with a gigantic bunch of lilies.

Apart from this new approach to drama criticism, I think you also wrote a play around that time, didn't you?

There are certain youthful indiscretions which I'd rather we didn't talk about. More to the point is that I collected together all the poetry I'd been writing since Trinity and had it issued in a single volume – *Poems* by Oscar Wilde. My friends reviewed it favourably and my enemies unfavourably – that's what criticism is all about. One can never be too careful in the choice of one's enemies. *Punch* called it "Swinburne and water", which was unkind, but did have the good sense to start caricaturing me as an Apostle of Beauty and a leader of the Aesthetic Movement. Even if that didn't ensure immortality, at least it guaranteed notoriety.

One hears a lot about this "Aesthetic Movement". What was it exactly?

Almost an invention, and not quite a myth. It was, essentially, the quest for beauty and the cult of art for art's sake, but the public regarded it with suspicion because of what they saw as our posturings and affectation, so it was much caricatured in the press. We were protesting against the ugliness and materialism of the age. It wasn't really a movement in the sense that Romanticism was, or Impressionism. It was more of a label attached, sometimes not entirely to their liking, to certain writers or artists, starting with the Pre-Raphaelites and brought to an end, if indeed it lasted as long, by my scandal in 1895. But my association with it in 1881 was all I'd been waiting for, because it got me a lucrative lecture tour of America.

DISCOVERING AMERICA

In April 1881, Richard D'Oyly Carte produced a new Gilbert and Sullivan operetta, *Patience*, in London. It lampooned the Aesthetic Movement, and one of the main characters, Bunthorne, although not a direct caricature of Oscar Wilde, had distinctly recognizable elements of him. When the show opened in the USA in September, Carte thought it would be a masterstroke to ship over a "live" aesthete to give a series of lectures and so provide the Americans with an embodiment of what the show was satirizing.

What were your first thoughts when Carte approached you? He wasn't exactly proposing the sort of Grand Tour that Thackeray had made as an established novelist, was he? This could well have been a poisoned chalice.

Poison and perfection, just like so many other things in my life. But the problem was whether I could apply the antidote to the one and survive to take advantage of the other. On my arrival in New York harbour, I was besieged by reporters, and I was as little prepared for them as they were for me. Curious though this may sound, despite my pursuit of publicity in London I'd never been subjected to that sort of journalism, which was eager to report – and did – every trivial sentence I uttered. I think they were expecting a Niagara of epigrams and didn't get it, so even a chance remark I'd made to another passenger on the voyage over was turned into a headline: MR WILDE DISAPPOINTED WITH THE ATLANTIC. But I more than made up for it the following day by announcing to the customs official that I had nothing to declare but my genius. For one uneasy moment, I thought he was going to levy duty on it as a rare foreign commodity.

New York fêted you in a way you could only have dreamed of back in London.

It certainly did. I was torn in bits by Society — there had been nothing like this since Dickens, they told me. There were immense receptions, where for two hours the New Yorkers filed past for introductions. I bowed graciously and sometimes honoured them with a royal observation, which appeared next day in all the newspapers. Crowds waited for my carriage. I waved a gloved hand and an ivory cane and they cheered. Rooms were hung with white lilies for me everywhere. I had two secretaries. One was there to write my autograph and answer the hundreds of letters that came begging for it. Another, whose hair was brown, sent locks of his own hair to the young ladies who wrote asking for mine. He rapidly became bald. As a lover of virtuous obscurity, you can imagine how much I disliked all the lionizing.

Oh yes, naturally — a terrible ordeal for you, I'm sure. And this wasn't really what you had come to do, was it?

It was all useful preparation once I'd mastered the press. But you're right: I was there to lecture and my idea was to show, believe it or not, a certain seriousness of intent. That was to be the antidote I needed to disperse the cloud of misrepresentation that preceded me, and the "greenery-yallery Grosvenor Gallery, flippety-flop young man" image of *Patience* quite simply had to go. So I lectured on what I called the new Renaissance of English Art and its origins in 2,000 years of European culture. It wasn't at all what they'd expected, which was some sort of music-hall turn, but to me it was an excellent example of the fact that we had everything in common with America, except, of course, civilization. This was a nation in a hurry, not a state of mind favourable to poetry or romance – imagine Romeo or Juliet in a constant state of anxiety about trains and return tickets. What interested practical America was what it should do about its own arts and crafts and how people should decorate their homes. So I abandoned art history for interior design and became an immediate success.

**You weren't normally one for making
compromises.**

I prefer to think of it as a temporary victory for
the empirical over the impracticable, and as a
result the farthest corners of North America
wanted to hear my views on almost anything.
My tour was extended from six months to a
whole year. I lectured on Irish poets to the San
Franciscans in California, which was just like
Italy without its art. I lectured to silver miners in
Leadville about the Florentine silversmith Cellini
and was reproved for not having brought him
with me. When I explained that he'd been dead
for a while, they asked in their forthright manner,
"Who shot him?" I came to admire the Americans
not a little for their refreshing openness and their
strange charm, and they provided me with a fine
store of epigrams from then on – frequently, I
may say, to their advantage. And my American
tour also made me see, practically, the importance
of art as a refining influence in life, and that, too,
I worked into a lecture.

ALMOST
RESPECTABLE

Oscar returned to London at the end of 1882, having spent a whole year touring the United States. He came back an experienced lecturer and some $6,000 the richer (equivalent to £100,000 or $130,000 today). In his absence the English press, he was pleased to find, had widely reported his American cultural antics, and he immediately took advantage of this by arranging a series of similar lectures on home territory – "Personal Impressions of America", "Dress" and "The Value of Art in Modern Life". In 1884 Oscar married, and for two years from 1887 edited a monthly magazine, *Woman's World*, which brought in a regular income to support his young family.

There are a number of photographs taken of
you at the start of that American tour which,
I would say, have determined unshakably how
people have perceived you ever since — long
hair, fur coat, velvet jacket and knee-breeches,
looking every inch the aesthete and the dandy.
Are you happy that we should still see you
like that?

(*Laughs*) Well, I dare say it's the nearest I shall
come to being Dorian Gray, even if it's only in
the public imagination. I always used to say
that there was nothing I wouldn't do to regain
my youth except take exercise, get up early or
be respectable, and photography seems to have
done it all for me. In reality, though, by the time
I came back, I was ready to move on. All that
belonged to the Oscar of the first period, so I
had my hair cut, wore the clothes of any well-
dressed man of the time and moved Oscar into
the second period. It had more to do with words
than images. Dandies, in my experience, have
little time for anything other than being dandies,
and I was determined to have literary success. So
I went to Paris for a few months to write a play
which had been commissioned when I was in

America. When it was finished, the actress turned it down. I have to admit it wasn't the best thing I ever wrote, but another eight years passed before I could bring myself to write another. I then went back to London and set myself up touring Britain as a lecturer on America, Art and Dress. It was repetitive, tiring and, apart from the money, thoroughly unrewarding work, civilizing the provinces like that.

You used to say that literary writing, as opposed to journalism or reviewing, needed leisure, and freedom from sordid considerations like money – no hungry playwrights in garrets, then, no *vie de Bohème*?

Certainly not. The best work is always done by those who don't depend upon it for their daily bread, and the highest form of literature, poetry, brings no wealth to the singer at all. Quite apart from that, I couldn't do any real literary work while flying from one railway station to another. Then quite suddenly my whole life changed. I went to lecture in Dublin and decided that I was in love with someone whom I'd met before going to America. She was a young girl called

Constance Lloyd, a grave, slight, violet-eyed little Artemis, with great coils of heavy brown hair which made her flower-like head droop like a blossom. Her wonderful ivory hands drew music from the piano so sweet that the birds stopped singing to listen to her.

How very romantic. So you proposed, dazzled by all this beauty, and she accepted. It sounds a little like something I read somewhere ... how does it go? "Men marry because they are tired; women, because they are curious; both are disappointed." And a dowry, an inheritance, her prospects never crossed your mind?

I think you're being unnecessarily cynical. Delightful as cynicism is from its intellectual side, it can never be more than the perfect philosophy for a man who has no soul. To the true cynic nothing is ever revealed. I could have done a great deal better for myself financially, so please stop trying to apply what I take to be the standards of your age to mine. Of course, dowries and marriage settlements existed, and her grandfather put some capital in trust for her to help us start off, but none of this determined how we felt about each other. We were in love. And anticipating your next question — no, it wasn't to conceal my sexual preferences either. Anyway, the law on gross indecency wasn't passed until the following year.

Well, in view of all that happened later, people have wondered, and I'd have had to ask. So you got married. Apart from lecturing, how did you pay the bills?

With difficulty. But then it's only by not paying one's bills that one can ever hope to live in the memory of the commercial classes. I descended to journalism, largely reviewing books and the like. I took far more care than was necessary with the pieces I did, and it seems they caught the eye of a publisher, who asked me to edit a woman's magazine. It was exactly what I needed — a regular income and a new entrée into Society. *Punch* had ignored me for two years, and if there's one thing worse than being talked about, it's not being talked about.

...have they not. And now, don't you,
I think we should say this nice young man who
has looked after us so admirably all afternoon.

SHOCKING THE MIDDLE CLASSES

Reinventing himself for the third time since leaving Oxford, in 1889 Oscar started on the great creative period of his life. During this time he wrote most of the works for which he is remembered today, including his only novel, *The Picture of Dorian Gray*, and all his major plays: *Lady Windermere's Fan*, *A Woman of No Importance*, *An Ideal Husband* and *The Importance of Being Earnest*. The metamorphosis of Oscar Wilde from languid aesthete with lily to sharp-witted playwright with green carnation was almost complete.

I think it was about this time that you must have realized you were hovering on the edge of that bourgeois respectability which you so scorned. There you were, married with two children, editing a woman's magazine, reviewing books and with just a few short stories and a collection of fairy tales for children to your name. Didn't that worry you?

In a word – yes. Naturally, as the father of a family I had responsibilities. I even applied to become an Inspector of Schools again, but I was refused. All for the best, probably, as the effect on English education could have been startling. I began to think it one of the great truths of modern life that unless one was wealthy there was no use in being a charming fellow, and maybe it would be better for me to have a permanent income than to be fascinating. But fortunately this was only a fleeting thought, a momentary deviation, as I also realized that domesticity ages one rapidly, and distracts one's mind from higher things. I needed the stimulus of Society for my work, and to get into the best Society I had to feed people, to amuse people or to shock people. The first was impossible, as our grocer had withdrawn all credit, and the second I'd already been doing for years. So the time had come for the third, to play Baudelaire to the English middle-classes – *épater le bourgeois*, as he loved to say.

So where did you start – with *The Picture of Dorian Gray*?

Well, that was how it was later perceived – my first full-length novel becoming an instant *succès de scandale*. I was even accused by one critic of writing for "outlawed noblemen and perverted telegraph boys", though he did have the intelligence to call it "ingenious and plainly the work of a man of letters". I was delighted to have been attacked so roundly: praise makes me humble, but when I'm abused, I know I have touched the stars. But, you know, *Dorian Gray* wasn't the first broadside I fired at the literary establishment. About 18 months before, I'd published an essay in the form of a dialogue, which I called "The Decay of Lying" – the title alone was designed to irritate my contemporaries.

Did you write it purely to provoke, or did it have a serious message?

What a dreadful idea that I might have written anything with a message, but at least it's better than writing something with a moral. If you insist on a description, I'd say that beneath the fanciful dialogue there were some truths about the state of modern literature which needed to be put forward. The ancient historians used to give us delightful fiction in the form of fact, but the modern novelist was presenting us with dull facts under the guise of fiction. Promising young writers with a natural gift for exaggeration were, in no time, developing a morbid and unhealthy habit of truth-telling, and ending up writing novels which were so lifelike that no one could possibly believe in them. The revolting sentimentality of the three-volume novel was a case in point, so I made a plea for a return to the art of telling beautiful and untrue things – that noble and lost art of Lying. Well, of course, having made the proposal, I had to show that it could be done, which is how I came to write *Dorian Gray*.

So you blew a breath of fresh air into the English novel.

Perhaps — I think I'd rather call it a breath of very different air. It was a book dealing with the worship of the senses, which the English, with their instinctive terror about passions and sensations that seem stronger than themselves, have never really understood. Victorian England tried to starve those feelings into submission or to kill them by pain, instead of making them, as I was, elements of a new spirituality. But you could hardly expect otherwise from a nation which has such a miraculous power to turn wine into water.

Did you have any idea of the uproar the story would cause when it appeared?

I knew there would be disapproval, but I could never have foreseen the extent of it. Quite remarkable — and, of course, very satisfying. Naturally, I stoked the fire for as long as I could with replies to the critics, especially those who committed the unpardonable crime of trying to confuse the artist with his subject matter and to imply that the author was as immoral as his characters. I remember my wife, poor thing, saying at the time, "Since Oscar wrote *Dorian Gray*, no one will speak to us."

FEASTING WITH PANTHERS

"Give a man a mask and he will tell you the truth," said Oscar Wilde, and this aphorism could certainly be applied to his own life. Sometime around 1887, it is generally accepted, he became a practising homosexual. Robbie Ross, later to prove his staunchest friend (and subsequently his literary executor), was probably his first male lover, followed by one or two others until the arrival in his life of Lord Alfred Douglas (Bosie, as he was nicknamed by his family and close friends) in 1891. Oscar's wife, Constance, does not appear to have had any suspicions about his extra-marital liaisons until a few months before his trials. The theme of concealment is increasingly evident in his work.

I'm going to ask you another indiscreet question. Was Robbie Ross the first man with whom you had an affair?

Questions are never indiscreet, but answers sometimes are, and you seem to have a perfectly disgusting appetite for facts. Let's just say I wouldn't have minded if he had been.

All right, I won't press the point, but it seems to have been around that time that you realized your attraction to young men wasn't ... well, just platonic.

In married life three is company and two is none. Married life was duller than I'd anticipated and I wanted to experience new sensations. I didn't want to be at the mercy of my emotions – I wanted to use them, to enjoy them, to dominate them. It opened a new, a forbidden world and, heaven knows, there were enough people in high places doing the same thing. One just didn't advertise the fact. At first it was passing affairs with young writers and poets, but after I'd been introduced to Alfred Douglas, things became very different – he had connections in the *demi-monde* of London. Tired of being on the heights, I deliberately went to the depths in the search for new sensations. What the paradox was to me in the sphere of thought, perversity became to me in the sphere of passion. I entertained rent boys and blackmailers at dinner and found pleasure in their company. It was like feasting with panthers. The danger was half the excitement, their poison part of their perfection. I became the spendthrift of my own genius, and to waste an eternal youth gave me a curious joy.

Just now, when we were talking about *Dorian Gray*, you said that the critics had behaved badly by trying to associate your personal life with your subject matter, but from all you say, they came quite close to the truth.

I admit that it made me slightly uncomfortable, but it would have been pure conjecture on their part. My relationships were not conducted openly then – not like my affair with Bosie later on. I sometimes forget it myself, but I wrote *The Picture of Dorian Gray* nearly two years before Bosie and I first met, so of course the story couldn't be about my relationship with him. If anything, it was my unfortunate destiny, as I'd argued in "The Decay of Lying", to illustrate the unerring instinct of Life to imitate Art. As I wrote to someone a little later, "That strange coloured book of mine contains much of me in it. Basil Hallward is what I think I am; Lord Henry what the world thinks me; Dorian what I would like to be – in other ages, perhaps."

You'd have to admit, though, that the double life you were forced to lead and the element of secrecy are quite strongly reflected in your work. You yourself once wrote in a review of a biography of Keats that the facts of his life were interesting only when they were shown in their relation to his creative activity – in isolation they were either uninteresting or painful.

Oh dear, yes. I'd forgotten that. Being tripped up by one's past is the price one pays for immortality, I suppose. But do we have to dwell on all this cause and effect? It was the clash of my two worlds, certainly, that produced some of my best work. Let's talk about the plays themselves. Why don't you ask me if I had in mind the Aristotelian dramatic unities when I was writing them?

Well, did you?

(*Laughs*) No, certainly not. But once *Lady Windermere's Fan* had been produced and had been an extraordinary success, I realized that writing modern drawing room plays with pink lampshades, seasoned with epigrams, and gently mocking the established order, was a formula which I could reproduce with variations. In addition, miraculously, theatre managers were happy to pay me large amounts of money, most of which I seemed to spend on my financially ruinous dalliance with Bosie.

So was there any artistic satisfaction in all this?

But of course: instant recognition and applause by the largest drawing room in London – the West End stage.

A FATAL FRIENDSHIP

Contrary to appearances, the relationship between Oscar Wilde and Lord Alfred Douglas was not that of an older man leading a younger man astray. Douglas, the third son of the Marquess of Queensberry, had already had homosexual relationships while a student at Oxford, and it was as a result of a blackmailing attempt over one of his liaisons that he appealed to Oscar for help. Oscar, who had already met Bosie several times and was attracted by his exceptional good looks, and initially also by his title and the poetry he wrote, found the appeal irresistible ... and that, as he later described in *De Profundis*, was where it all began.

For nearly three years after you had your first great stage success with *Lady Windermere's Fan*, you and Alfred Douglas had been more or less inseparable, hadn't you?

No, not quite. It was a stormy relationship at best. It pains me to say so, but it was essentially an unintellectual friendship, a friendship whose primary aim was not the creation and contemplation of beautiful things, and I allowed it to dominate my life entirely. Bosie's interests were in his meals and his moods, in amusements and pleasures. He had no motives in life — merely appetites. He admired my work when it was finished. He enjoyed the brilliant successes of my first nights, and the brilliant banquets that followed them, but while he was by my side I hardly wrote a single line. My life was sterile and uncreative. Nevertheless, there were qualities which I loved in him, and although he may not have been my literary muse, he was certainly a delightful distraction — delightful, that is, until he lost control of his tongue and his emotions, and made terrible scenes and wrote me revolting and loathsome letters. It was a dreadful mania he inherited from his father. Of course, these outbursts were always followed by remorse and reconciliation. One had either to give in to him or to give him up, and I gave in — always. There were times when I remember thinking what an impossible, terrible, utterly wrong state my life had got into.

Things were hardly improved by Queensberry, were they?

No. Bosie's father was an irascible aristocrat — he'd mistreated his wife and quarrelled with all his children. Francis, his eldest son and heir, had been appointed Private Secretary to Lord Rosebery in the Foreign Office at about the time Bosie and I first met, and Queensberry suspected that their relationship was "private" in more senses than just the official one. He wasn't best pleased by the idea, so the open secret in London that his third son had formed a romantic attachment to Oscar Wilde, "the high priest of decadence", he found intolerable. He and I met by chance on a couple of occasions when I was lunching with Bosie in the Café Royal, and both times we parted on friendly terms. But he was soon writing to Bosie about our filthy, disgusting relationship and threatening to horsewhip him if he caught us together in public. Bosie acquired a revolver and said that if his father did lay hands on him so, he'd shoot him in self-defence. That was the appalling state of things by the summer of 1894.

So the threats were made to Bosie rather than to you?

To begin with, yes. But sometime that summer – it was towards the end of June, I think – his father turned up at my house in Tite Street with a dangerous-looking rough. I thought the best course of action was righteous indignation, so I asked if he'd come to apologize for the public remarks he was making about his son and me. It wasn't perhaps the most diplomatic thing to do, as it unleashed from Queensberry a torrent of foul-mouthed abuse about my relationship with Bosie and what he called a "disgusting sodomitic letter" that I'd written to his son. That was unfortunate, and I've no idea how he'd heard about it, but I had indeed written Bosie a beautiful letter about a sonnet he'd sent me, and Bosie had been careless enough to leave it in a suit of clothes he'd given

away. London being London, blackmailers had
soon appeared on my doorstep, but I'd managed
to sort things out and thought that would be the
end of it — yet here was Queensberry dragging the
whole business up again. When I asked him if he
was accusing Bosie and me of sodomy, he replied,
"I don't say that you are it, but you look it and you
pose as it, which is just as bad", and threatened
to thrash me if he ever found us together again.
"I don't know what the Queensberry rules are,"
I said, "but the Oscar Wilde rule is to shoot on
sight. Please leave my house at once."

Eventually he did leave, his face distorted
with rage and chattering like a monstrous ape.
I couldn't help thinking, for the briefest of
moments and with a feeling of absolute horror,
how much father and son resembled each other
in their fury.

**Wasn't that one of the times when cold reason
told you that you must extricate yourself before
you became the dupe in this terrible father-and-
son battle?**

Became? I was already. That autumn, when I was
ill at Brighton, Bosie made the most hideous scene

I can remember. He left for London and two days later, on my birthday, I received a letter from him which I imagined would be full of the usual pretty phrases of regret. I had underestimated him: it was an elaborate repetition of all the hateful words he'd used a few days before, and concluded, "When you are not on your pedestal you are not interesting. The next time you are ill I will go away at once." I felt a strange sense of relief knowing that the ultimate moment had come, and that for the sake of my art and my life I could now take steps to be free both of him and of his father. But it wasn't to be. Shortly after, I learned that his eldest brother had died in a shooting accident and, forgetting his revolting behaviour to me, I extended my hand, my heart, in sympathy. The gods are strange. It's not of our vices only that they make instruments to scourge us — they bring us to ruin through what in us is good, gentle, humane, loving. But for my pity and affection for Bosie at that terrible moment, I could have shaken his insane, divided family out of my life forever.

Couldn't you at least have got some sort of court order restraining Queensberry?

Well, I needed him to make a spectacle of himself again, and I didn't have to wait long. On the first night of *The Importance of Being Earnest* he tried to buy a ticket so that he could address the audience about the morals of the playwright. When we prevented that, he tried to gain entrance by the stage door with a grotesque bouquet of vegetables. There he was stopped by the police, who had been alerted to his intentions. Finally he left in a foul temper, and some days later left his card with the hall porter of my club. On it he'd written, "For Oscar Wilde, posing somdomite" – spelling wasn't one of his lordship's strongest suits. As I wrote to Robbie, I could see nothing left but a criminal prosecution.

THE LIBEL TRIAL

As so often in Oscar's life, at this point he was pulled in two directions by conflicting forces: his head and his heart, represented by Robbie Ross and Bosie Douglas. Significantly, on the evening he received the Marquess's card, he wrote to Robbie asking him to come to the Avondale Hotel at 11:30 that night and saying that he had asked Bosie to come the next day. Instinctively he knew that Ross's practical and sensible advice was what he needed. However, by the time Ross arrived, Bosie was already there working his sorcery: Oscar was soon persuaded to embark on a disastrous libel action.

**When you look back to those extraordinary
first months of 1895, to the huge success of *An
Ideal Husband* and *The Importance of Being
Earnest* both running to packed houses in
London's West End, don't you sometimes ask
yourself what madness it was that provoked you
into suing Bosie's father for leaving that card at
your club?**

Of course it was madness, but there were so many
reasons for my madness that I couldn't see a
single one of them. I'd allowed the heady wine of
success to blind me to the dangers of appealing to
the law, when in reality I myself had been living
in defiance of the law for several years. But I felt
that the gods had given me almost everything.
I had genius, a distinguished name, high social
position, brilliancy, intellectual daring. I made art
a philosophy, and philosophy an art. I altered the
minds of men and the colours of things – there
was nothing I said or did that didn't make people
wonder. I awoke the imagination of my century
so that it created myth and legend around me.
I summed up all systems in a phrase, and all
existence in an epigram. Can it surprise you that I
had no fear of failure?

Weren't there friends who warned you that what you were doing was suicidal?

Yes, there were. Robbie came to see me on the very evening I received the card and pressed me to ignore it. Bosie, with all the aggression of that mad, bad line from which he came, and consumed by hatred for his father, wanted nothing more than to see him behind bars, or at least in the dock. His hatred was so suffocating that it entirely outstripped and overshadowed his love of me. There's no room for both those passions in the same soul. Love is fed by the imagination, by which we become wiser than we know, better than we feel, nobler than we are. Only what is fine, and finely conceived, can feed Love, but anything will feed Hate, as I discovered at terrible cost to myself. From that moment I allowed Bosie to dominate me, and his father to frighten me. I ceased to be lord over myself. I was no longer the Captain of my Soul, and didn't know it. We went the very next day to the magistrate's court and applied for a warrant to have Bosie's father arrested for criminal libel.

Surely, though, you could still have withdrawn from the prosecution at any time?

Naturally, as the prosecutor, it was up to me to determine the course of things — or it would have been, except that my willpower became absolutely subject to Bosie's. It sounds a grotesque thing to say, I know, but it's none the less true. It was the triumph of the smaller over the bigger nature — that tyranny of the weak over the strong which somewhere in one of my plays I describe as being "the only tyranny that lasts". I can remember meeting Frank Harris and Bernard Shaw in the Café Royal shortly before the case came on. They were both adamant that to continue was sheer folly, as no jury in England would convict a father for apparently protecting his son from me.

But the main aim of the "screaming scarlet Marquess", as you called him, wasn't to protect his son — he simply wanted to destroy you by provoking you into taking legal action against him.

I know, I know — but I didn't see it at the time. I loved Bosie. I wanted to please him, to help him in his dreadful game of hate with his father, and by the time I realized that they were throwing dice for my soul, it was too late. Ten days after having his father arrested, Bosie persuaded me to go off on holiday with him to Monte Carlo, when I should have been calmly considering the hideous trap in which I'd been caught. On our return, the Marquess's lawyers had prepared their plea of justification. I confess I was horrified by all that they'd discovered — extorted, more probably, by bribery and threats of prosecution — from the young blackmailers and rent boys.

And was it all true?

It was the truth that one buys for 30 pieces of silver.

Obviously more effective than the silence one buys with silver cigarette cases.

That's hardly fair. It was my habit to give cigarette cases to young people I liked. I enjoyed their company and I wanted them to have the pleasure of owning something which they wouldn't have been able to buy otherwise. I couldn't have foreseen that Queensberry's men would track them all down and take statements from each of them about their ... well, their private lives. The loyalty of the lower orders, I discovered, was as negotiable as the morals of the aristocracy.

Oddly enough, it wasn't really their testimony I was worried about. Almost all of it was uncorroborated and half of them had criminal records anyway. It would have been their word against mine. No, it was the attack on my work which roused my anger and made me careless of the danger. *Dorian Gray* was described in the plea as an immoral and obscene work dealing with sodomitical and unnatural practices, and I was being held up as a monster of vice and depravity for having written it. I suppose, looking back on it, I saw myself in the role of two of my great heroes of French literature, Baudelaire and Flaubert, defending my art against the philistines and the illiterate. They'd both been prosecuted by the French state, and although I wasn't being prosecuted, I certainly felt persecuted. Where better to make myself heard than in open court in a very public libel trial?

So you went into court confident that you'd succeed?

I was confident that I'd be able to carry the jury by showing how absurd it was to insinuate that I was guilty of Dorian Gray's unnamed sins simply because I'd written about them, and not even explicitly at that. I was sure that we would discredit the evidence of the defence witnesses. And I certainly felt that if my relationship with Bosie were brought up, there was no one who could possibly prove any "gross indecency", as the law quaintly called it, between us.

There were a few surprises in store, though, weren't there? You must have thought that Edward Carson, formidable advocate that he was, would have a trick or two up his sleeve.

Not really. I was quite amused to think that old Ned Carson would be appearing for the defence. I hadn't seen him since our days together at Trinity, where he didn't exactly distinguish himself intellectually, but I could imagine him conducting his side of the case with all the added bitterness of an old friend. I treated the whole affair as though it were some kind of elaborate game or even a piece of theatre. I had written the prologue, I had given myself the lead role, but I had no idea of the outcome. Imagine: an unscripted public performance at the Old Bailey. It was a delightful idea. I would play to the public gallery in an impromptu performance scattered with just enough witticisms to be humorous rather than frivolous. I suppose I had a wild hope that I might disarm destiny with laughter, though as a partial pagan I should have had a little more respect for the power of the Fates – and stuck to writing dramas rather than trying to act out my own.

The audience was a jury of shopkeepers who listened, bored and bewildered, to the finer points of my views on Literature and Morality. Then I thought I could make light of the cross-examination about the young men I'd entertained. I said that it was vulgar and snobbish to worry about social position – that was a mistake. When asked if I had kissed one of Bosie's servants at Oxford, I said rather flippantly "Oh no. He was a peculiarly plain boy." That was a disaster. I'd gone in to fight for my art and found myself fighting for my life.

You severely underestimated Carson's ability, I think you'd admit. He was as tenacious as a terrier, and by the time he opened for the defence, it was almost as if you were in the dock and not Queensberry.

It's strange you should say that — that's exactly what I felt after the second day in court. Ned Carson clearly found the idea that love could be expressed between two men distasteful, if not disgusting, and the law said it was illegal. But almost worse than that was the fact that I'd betrayed the conventions of my class — his class — and openly stated that I cared nothing for such distinctions. To entertain a groom, a valet or a newspaper boy was an astounding adventure. I think Carson found that intolerable, and it showed. How could anyone of my standing invite such people even just to dine with him? By the time it was clear he was going to bring those young men one by one into court and examine them, my own counsel told me to withdraw from the case before any more damage was done. But I still think we could have brazened it out.

DECADENCE
DISCREDITED

Oscar's libel action against the Marquess of Queensberry was halted shortly before lunch on the third day. Queensberry, characteristically vindictive, told his lawyers to send all their papers, which included statements from the rent boys and blackmailers, straight to the Director of Public Prosecutions. This done, the Government had no alternative but to prosecute Wilde, and he was arrested the same evening. Bail was refused and his trial followed three weeks later, ending inconclusively with a hung jury. A second trial was ordered, as a result of which Wilde was convicted of homosexual practices and sentenced to two years with hard labour.

Between the collapse of your case against Queensberry and your final conviction, you had several opportunities to go abroad and escape the consequences of your folly. Why didn't you?

Yes, I could have done. When I was eventually released on bail, several people, including my wife, suggested that I leave. But I'd been abroad twice already that year and to have gone abroad again would have made me look like a missionary, or what amounts to the same thing, a commercial traveller.

Please, Oscar, this is hardly the moment for being frivolous — we're talking about one of the turning points in your life.

My dear fellow, I am never more serious than when I'm treating life with frivolity – it's the only thing that makes it endurable. However, since you insist on a plausible explanation, I shall do my best to invent one. Let's see ... well, in the first place there was my poor mother. She'd taken such pride in my theatrical triumphs and was amused to see her son carrying on the family tradition of

tweaking John Bull's nose. That was fine as far
as it went. Even my getting on the wrong side of
the law didn't worry her unduly. After all, she'd
almost found herself in prison nearly 50 years
before, although that had been for high-minded
patriotism, and my trouble was a sordid little
scandal. Her view was that the nature of the
difficulty was unimportant so long as I conducted
myself as befitted an Irish gentleman. "If you stay,"
she said to me, "even if you go to prison, you will
always be my son. It will make no difference to my
affection. But if you go, I will never speak to you
again." That was a great comfort to me to know.

But you didn't stay just to please her, did you?

No, my mind was already made up. I would
stay and take the consequences. I even wrote
to the *Evening News* to say so, and since the
newspapers of my time pretended to exercise
a monopoly on the truth, I was bound to
be believed. There seemed to be something
inevitable about the whole affair from then on,
and if my destiny was to be disgrace and ruin, I
was going to play the part in style. Chance might
still have spared me, but I wasn't counting on it.

I had to experience the part of the tragic hero. Nemesis had caught me in her net – to struggle would have been foolish. Why is it that one runs to one's ruin? Why has destruction such a fascination? Why, when one stands on a pinnacle, *must* one throw oneself down? No one knows, but these things are so. Euripides would have been proud of my role – you see the appalling result of a good classical education. When the gods wish to punish us, they answer our prayers.

From where we stand today, it looks as though the English establishment was determined to make a spectacle of you. At first you were allowed no bail for what was designated only a misdemeanour. And then in the second trial you were prosecuted by the Solicitor-General himself, whose job, normally, was to take the most serious crimes like treason and murder.

I suppose I was the ideal scapegoat. The English disapproved of *Dorian Gray*, they disapproved of *Salomé*, and they thoroughly disapproved of me and all I stood for – the English Decadence, I suppose you could call it – but there was very little they could do about it. I was a rebel who

called into question something very dangerous —
the hypocrisy of those social, sexual and literary
values upon which Victorian society was so firmly
based. I cast a rainbow of forbidden colours
over a drab age of industrial power. I pushed my
subversive ideas and my subversive behaviour to
the limits of what they could tolerate — and then
just a little further, which they couldn't. It simply
wasn't playing the game, and it wasn't the stuff
that Empire builders were made of.

In addition to all that, there had been one
or two nasty scandals of a sexual nature in
recent years which, for various reasons, the
Government hadn't dealt with as firmly as the
public had expected. So it must have been an
enormous relief for them to discover that I'd
broken the law. Imagine — a perfect opportunity
to put me away to show that the Government
was defending public morals, as much as it was
defending that stalwart of English fiction, the
sentimental three-volume novel.

**Was there, bound up in all this, any thought that
you might become, even wanted to become, the
first martyr for the homosexual cause?**

Well, if I did become such a martyr, it was in spite of myself. My art to me was everything, the great primal note by which I'd revealed, first myself to myself, and then myself to the world. It was the real passion of my life, the love to which all other loves were as marsh-water to red wine, or the glow-worm of the marsh to the magic mirror of the moon. I was far too self-centred, I admit, to have been a dedicated reformer for anything before I went to prison, let alone to have consciously sacrificed my art and my freedom in protest against the law which finally sent me there.

Had I known then what I know now, and had I known the terrible price society would exact from me, I wonder sometimes whether I should ever have stood up for my art and my beliefs. True, the experience of prison made me see my life afterwards in a very different light, and for that at least I have to be grateful. And if, as you seem to be saying, "The Case of Oscar Wilde" – good heavens, the one I so innocently wished for all those years ago at school – has had the slightest effect on public opinion, well, some good *has* come of it all. But martyrdom, in all its pathetic uselessness, all its wasted beauty – never.

THE ARTIST IN PRISON

Oscar started his two-year sentence in Pentonville (north London), was moved after a couple of months to Wandsworth (south London) and spent the last year and a half in Reading Gaol. While in Wandsworth he was declared bankrupt. Prison conditions at the time were appalling: solitary confinement; no proper sanitation in the cells; minimal, almost inedible food; writing materials allowed only for official correspondence, petitions and a ration of four personal letters a year; and a literary diet of the few morally uplifting books kept in the prison libraries. Later, however, Oscar was allowed readable books, pen and paper, and he wrote the powerful letter to Alfred Douglas which was posthumously named *De Profundis*.

Nothing could possibly have prepared you for the experience of prison. You had written about criminals from a sort of romantic point of view – Wainewright the poisoner and Chatterton the forger – fascinated as you were by both of them. In *Dorian Gray* you wrote about the East End of London and the opium dens, and doubtless visited them, but always knowing that you could go home to your own bed.

Curious as it may seem, it wasn't my freedom I missed most, but those things I had taken for granted in my life – fine food, well-tailored clothes, writing materials and conversation. By contrast, the eternal silence, the hunger, the sleeplessness, the cruelty, the harsh and revolting punishments, the utter despair, the ignoble dress and the loathsome mode of life – they were terrible. In prison, suffering is one long moment, just as tears are a part of every day's experience. A day in prison on which you do not weep is a day on which your heart is hard, not a day on which your heart is happy. Of course, I missed my freedom, too. The very sun and moon seem taken from you. Outside, the day may be blue and gold, but the light that creeps down through the thickly

muffled glass of the small iron-barred window
beneath which you sit is grey and niggard. It
is always twilight in your cell, as it is always
midnight in your heart.

**The solitude and endless time to reflect on
what you'd done must inevitably have changed
your feelings about Bosie.**

When I thought about the letter I'd written to
him, while I was on remand in Holloway Prison,
assuring him of my eternal love, and realized
just where that love had brought me, you can
imagine that a certain bitterness took its place.
There was something hugely ironical, too, in
the idea that it wasn't really Bosie who had put
me into prison, nor even his father. Neither
of them, multiplied 1,000 times over, could
possibly have ruined a man like me – I had
ruined myself. Terrible as what they did to me
was, what I did to myself was far more terrible
still. And it wasn't just what I'd done to myself.
The contents of my home were auctioned off
by the bailiffs to pay my debts, my wife had
to go abroad with the children, Queensberry
bankrupted me for his costs in the libel trial,

and the disgrace which I'd brought on myself, I brought on my whole family. Worse, even, was the effect on my dearest mother. She and my father had bequeathed me a name they had made noble and honoured not merely in Literature, Art, Archaeology and Science, but in the history of Ireland's evolution as a nation. I had disgraced that name eternally. I still believe it was I who hastened her death by what I did. Her death was so terrible to me that I, once a lord of language, had no words in which to express my anguish and my shame.

She asked for you to be brought to her as she was dying, I believe, but it wasn't allowed.

No, and I learned the news from my wife who travelled, ill as she was, all the way from Italy to tell me, so that I shouldn't hear it from some stranger. She was gentle and good to me when she came to see me. She kissed me, she comforted me, she behaved as no woman in history, except my own mother perhaps, could have behaved. And that wasn't the first time – she'd come from abroad to see me once before to say that she was obliged, for the sake of the boys, to change her name, but that she wouldn't divorce me. On my release she would arrange to have an allowance paid to me and let me see my children twice a year. Afterwards she wrote me a very touching and affectionate letter. Everything, including our marriage settlement, was sorted out in the most amicable fashion, until my friends, in a misguided attempt to claim more on my behalf, started making mischief between us. Why couldn't people have left us alone to sort out our lives?

I think your life at that moment, full of anger, anguish and bitterness as it was, and no outlet for any of it, must have pushed you to the brink of sanity.

It did, except that, at last, I'd been allowed paper and a pen. Before I had them, my brain had been going round in very evil circles. I started my great letter to Bosie, and with the mere fact of being able to write again, it was as if a great cleansing wave had washed away all the bitterness and the festering resentment of 18 months of silence and solitude. I treated it as a letter, *Epistola: In Carcere et Vinculis*, a letter from prison and in chains,* because the form suited what I had to say. I wasn't trying to defend my conduct of the past five years but to explain it, to give an account of my extraordinary behaviour with regard to Bosie and his father. In the end I wasn't allowed to send it, which was just as well because Bosie undoubtedly would have destroyed it in a fit of anger at all my reproaches. What was almost as important to me was that writing about my prison experience helped me to try and prepare for the outside world, to accept that I had been the common prisoner of a common gaol and teach myself not to be ashamed of it.

As an educated man you must have suffered more than others, but wouldn't you say you were fortunate in that respect? You could begin your own rehabilitation.

Yes, that's true. It was one of the great failings of the system and, for all I know, probably still is. Society inflicts appalling punishment on an individual and then abandons him at the very moment when its highest duty towards him

* First published (in part) in 1905 as *De Profundis*.

begins, at the moment the punishment is over. Many men on their release carry their prison along with them, hide it as a secret disgrace in their hearts, and at length like poor poisoned things creep into some hole and die. It is wretched that they should have to do so, and it is wrong, terribly wrong, of Society that it should force them to.

A SORT OF FREEDOM

Having served his full sentence without a day's remission or allowance for time in custody, Oscar was released on 19 May 1897 and went straight to France. He never set foot in England again. Constance sent money to help him make a new start, and agreed to make him a quarterly allowance. They wrote to each other planning to meet, but the meeting never took place. Oscar spent the summer at Berneval near Dieppe being visited by friends and initially resisting Bosie Douglas's advances. It was there that he completed his last work, *The Ballad of Reading Gaol*.

Just now, you talked of yourself as the tragic hero, bravely facing any ignominy you might have brought upon yourself, and yet the moment you were released you went into a sort of self-imposed exile like a whipped dog. Do you think your sentence destroyed a vital part of you?

When I came out of prison I was an ex-convict, a bankrupt and a homosexual. Do you have any idea what that meant? Any one of those labels was enough to make me a pariah in Victoria's England. There was nothing for it but to cross the Channel and try to remake my ruined life in France, mother to all artists that she is. I don't think prison destroyed anything other than what was bad in me. I'd been leading a life of senseless pleasure, of deliberate materialism – a life quite unworthy of the artist that I was. I learned many things in prison that were terrible to learn, but I learned some good lessons that I needed. Once free and in France, and in the company of friends, I felt I should be able to write again. There was a small reception committee of them at Dieppe to meet me off the

night boat. And — goodness, how Mrs Cheveley*
would have disapproved! — I was positively
brilliant at breakfast. The joy of conversing freely
again — that was a sheer delight. I wrote letters
by the dozen for a week; I wrote forcefully on
prison reform to the *Daily Chronicle*; I sent
money, the little that I could, to my fellow
prisoners in time for their release. Just the
handling of pen and paper again for pleasure
renewed my desire for life.

But my new home wasn't the home of my
friends, as London had been once, so one by
one they left and I began to realize my terrible
position of isolation. For one horrible day — the
first I'd spent on my own — I felt I had merely
exchanged one prison for another. Two long
years of silence had kept my soul in bonds. Now
I longed for the grace of sweet companionship,
the charm of pleasant conversation, and all those
gentle humanities that make life lovely.

**But surely you must have foreseen that? You
wrote movingly enough from prison about**

---

* Witty *femme fatale* from *An Ideal Husband* who declared, "Only
dull people are brilliant at breakfast."

Society's lack of interest in what happened to offenders on their release and what should be done to change it.

It is about as easy to mend the lives of others with wise words as it is impossible to set to rights one's own. What I wrote, I wrote about everyday criminals. I had more demands to make on life. You can put a poet in prison and destroy his health, but you'll never destroy his need for poetry. I began to realize, too, how much I'd relied on Society – the Society I'd mocked, whose face I'd shown reflected in a mirror so that it should see how grotesque it was – that Society had made me an outcast. I think that was why, in part, my wife and I never met again. You see, I was a problem for which there was no solution. How could Mrs Wilde, or Mrs Holland as she had now styled herself, associate with one as depraved as I was? What attitude were her family and friends to adopt socially on the rare occasions that we might meet? The simple thing was to keep us apart: "Give it time, my dear. A few months for him to adjust ..." And things were little better in Dieppe. It was easier to snub me than to risk being seen in my company.

So your feeling of increasing isolation in a small French coastal village wasn't exactly conducive to re-establishing yourself as a writer.

Of Society comedies? Hardly. I found myself gradually thinking that everything that had happened was for the best. This may have been philosophy, or a broken heart, or religion, or just the dull apathy of despair, but it made me deeply aware that I needed to transform my terrible experiences of the past two years into something spiritual, rather than pretend they hadn't happened. The atmosphere, though quite depressing, was ideal for that at least, and I started work on my *Ballad* – my swansong, as it turned out.

It could only be a temporary remedy, though. It wasn't going to cure the root cause of your unhappiness, was it?

No. Friends came to see me but their visits were fewer and fewer, and what I felt most was the loss of my children – that the law should have decided I was unfit to be with them was something quite horrible to me, and remained a source of infinite pain. And Robbie, dear sweet Robbie – I longed for his presence to comfort me. Lonely, dishonoured man, in disgrace and obscurity and poverty as I was, yet I was haunted by the idea that it would have been selfish to ask him to be with me.

Thirty years before, you wrote that your idea of misery was living a poor and respectable life in an obscure village. Do you remember that?

No, but that's certainly what it felt like.

I've an awful feeling I know what's coming next.

Look at my state of mind at the time. Can you blame me? There I was in Berneval, with the summer coming to an end. Mists, which Corot could have painted, rolled in from the Channel – does Life ever stop imitating Art? – and I was looking into a future bright with precisely nothing. I had very little money, and one day I nearly committed suicide, I was so bored. At that moment, Bosie came back into my life, offering me love, companionship and somewhere to live for the winter – Naples.

THE LAST ACT

The reunion was universally condemned by friends and families on both sides but, predictably, it didn't last. In December, Oscar and Bosie parted for good. The following spring saw the publication of the *Ballad*, and also the death of Oscar's wife, Constance, at the age of 40, from complications following an operation on her spine. With little left to live for and even less to live on, he spent his last three years partly in Paris and partly wandering somewhat aimlessly around Europe, cadging from the few friends who would still associate with him.

I can't understand how you could have gone back to Bosie after all that had happened. When you arrived in Berneval, you even said he was an evil influence and you hoped never to see him again. And you must have known how much disapproval, anger even, it would arouse among those who'd tried to help you back onto your feet.

My going back to Bosie was psychologically inevitable – the world forced it on me. I can't live without the atmosphere of Love. I must love and be loved, whatever price I pay for it. In my loneliness and disgrace, after three months' struggle against a hideous philistine world, I turned naturally to him. He was still the same wilful, fascinating, irritating, destructive, delightful personality, and of course I imagined that I should often be unhappy, but still I loved him – the mere fact that he'd wrecked my life made me love him. He meant well – I suppose he wanted to make amends for some of the suffering he'd caused me. But by living with me, he forfeited his allowance from his mother and I mine from Constance. After that, he expected me to provide for both of us, and

when I couldn't, he made one of his scenes.
We were finally starved into submission and he
had to leave. When I think of all the promises
he made, all the protestations of devotion and
how I should never want for anything, and then
the grim reality which followed, I see it was just
another fit of madness brought on by the love I
once felt for him. It was a blow quite awful and
paralysing – one of the most bitter experiences
of a bitter life. But I must admit that it cured me
of him for good.

**Getting to Paris, which was a city you knew well
and loved, and having your first book published
for nearly four years, must have made you feel
happier, didn't it?**

Well, on those occasions when I could actually
afford to eat, at least I no longer had to put up
with Neapolitan cooking, and being in Paris,
I felt, was my only chance of working again.
I missed an intellectual atmosphere, and the
French, even if they didn't embrace me with open
arms, at least tolerated my presence. My sexual
preferences were regarded in France as a perfectly
normal aberration. Having a book published,

though, really gave me a sense that I could produce something good once more. Did you see the title page? "The Ballad of Reading Gaol by C. 3. 3." – just my prison number, and my name nowhere to be seen. My publisher, Leonard Smithers, and I chose to do that partly so that the English public could buy the book without in any way associating themselves with the monster they perceived me to be, but partly also to say: "You have made a poet a convict – very well, here is the convict's poem."

But it sold well, and encouraged the publisher to do two more books with you, didn't it?

Smithers was a louche character – the most learned erotomaniac in Europe, I called him. He published Aubrey's* naughty drawings, that sort of thing. No one else would touch anything by me, and he paid me in five pound notes or the Official Receiver would have taken the money. Yes, he published *An Ideal Husband* and *The Importance*, which gave me a bit more to live on, but it was still my name that terrified – "By the

---

* Aubrey Beardsley (1872–1898), the decadent, often erotic artist who illustrated Wilde's *Salomé*.

author of *Lady Windermere's Fan*" was all he felt
we should say. My continuing existence was a
scandal. The irony was that I'd spent most of my
life wearing masks to deceive Life, and here was
Life obliging me to wear one so she shouldn't see
my face.

You and your wife never did make up your differences, did you?

You make it sound as if we didn't want to.
That was just another part of the continuing
tragedy. I'm not saying that we would have
lived together again — that would have been
highly improbable. She couldn't give me the
intellectual stimulus I needed and she knew
it, and anyway by then I was only attracted to
young men. But she was the mother of my two
boys. She knew of the deep affection between
me and my sons, and had even written to me
when I was in prison saying she hoped I might
win back the intellectual position I'd lost so
that, when they were older, they might be proud
to acknowledge me as their father. From the
moment other people started meddling in our
affairs, trying to do "the right thing" as they

kept calling it, financially when I was helpless in prison, and emotionally when I was released, it opened a gap between us which could never be closed. She died not long after the *Ballad* was published, and it was a year before I could visit her grave. It was tragic seeing her name carved on a tomb: her surname – my name – wasn't mentioned. Just "Constance Mary, daughter of Horace Lloyd." I was deeply affected with a sense of the uselessness of all regrets. If we had only met once and kissed each other ... I asked the children's guardian if I could write to them, but he told me that any attempt to contact them would be prevented and the letters destroyed.

Although her allowance to you continued afterwards, you led a fairly precarious existence, didn't you? I get the feeling that Constance's death marked the beginning of the end.

Solitude in a city like Paris is a terrible thing. I suddenly lost the mainspring of life and art, *la joie de vivre* – it was dreadful. I had pleasures, and passions, but the joy of life was gone. I felt I was going under – the morgue yawned for me.

I lived, or was supposed to live, on a few francs a day – a bare remnant saved from shipwreck. And as if my shattered mental state were not enough, an expanding waist added to my misery. Nothing fattens so much as a dinner at 1 franc 50. Like dear St Francis of Assisi I was wedded to Poverty, but in my case the marriage wasn't a success. I hadn't the soul of St Francis: my thirst was for the beauty of life, my desire for its joy, but I was living on echoes and had little music of my own. Imaginative writing meant letters to friends with new and untried excuses for borrowing money. I'd written all there was to write. I wrote when I didn't know life, and once I did know the meaning of life, I had no more to write. Life can't be written, life can only be lived, and I had lived – too well, you might say.

So you finally became a Catholic, didn't you?

Is that what they say? I do remember that Robbie always promised ... yes, that's right, he once arranged for a priest to come and see me about baptism. I was ill in bed at the time and could hardly talk, but when he asked if I wanted to be received into the Church of Rome, I felt I couldn't let the occasion pass without comment, so I raised my hand and ... well, I suppose he took it as a sign of assent. But you'd better not say anything ... I wouldn't have minded and it might ruin a good story.

AFTER OSCAR

On 30 November 1900, Oscar Wilde died of meningitis in Paris, having been received into the Catholic Church. He was given a pauper's burial in a leased grave outside the city. By 1906 Robbie Ross had collected enough money, largely from sales of a much-expurgated *De Profundis*, to purchase a permanent burial plot in Père Lachaise cemetery, where Oscar's remains were transferred in 1909. Such was his enduring infamy that it is said no child in England could be christened Oscar for years after his death. By contrast, on the Continent his posthumous reputation was soon assured, largely by *The Picture of Dorian Gray* and *Salomé*, the two works which could be said to have contributed to his downfall.

Regret is not a word with which one often associates you, but you must have had some regrets about the way your life turned out.

Well, if you'll allow me to distinguish between regret and remorse, it's a simple enough question to answer. I don't regret for a single moment having lived for pleasure. I did it to the full, as one should do everything one does to the full. There was no pleasure I didn't experience. I threw the pearl of my soul into a cup of wine. Nor do I regret refusing to accept the standards and the morality of my age — I consider that for any man of culture to accept the standards of his age is a form of the grossest *im*morality. My great mistake was that for too long I nurtured my body with a rich diet of sensuality and starved my soul of the simple fare it required. I wrote of pain and misery, of sorrow and despair, as though they were mere sensations, and I forgot that suffering is a terrible fire — it destroys but it also purifies. That was something the Greeks knew. It was something I'd known and something which, in my disgrace, I was forced to rediscover. It was a terrible lesson, but I can honestly say that I've no regrets on account of it. Most people die of a sort of creeping common sense, and discover when it's too late that the only things one should never regret are one's mistakes.

That's rather what you wrote to Bosie from prison, when you said that to reject one's own experiences is to arrest one's own development, and to deny one's own experiences is to put a lie into the lips of one's own life. Nevertheless, this was a pretty self-centred attitude.

It was the attitude of an artist whose principal aim in life was self-realization. Sometimes I used to think that the artistic life was a long and lovely suicide. Now I'm convinced of it, and I'm not sorry that it's so. My remorse, if you'll accept it as genuine after all I've said, was for the suffering and the pain I caused to those around me. Not the rent boys, who led wonderfully wicked lives and were perfectly capable of looking after themselves, nor Bosie, who survived my prison sentence with little worse than a few sleepless nights and nothing that his allowance of £400 a year couldn't cure. No, it was the innocents in the tragedy: my wife, my children, my mother, whose destinies had unwittingly become entangled with mine.

Although it may surprise you, I was really very fond of my wife, but I was bored to death with the married life and for years I disregarded the tie. She had some sweet points in her character, and was wonderfully loyal to me, even if she never really understood me. But by my disgrace I broke her heart, just as I broke my mother's, and although hearts are made to be broken, I'm eternally ashamed of having done it.

Come now, I've talked too much and one gets no receipt from the past by flattering it with remorse. We have drunk the sun to rest with wine and words – well, with coffee at least – and the evening has crept up on us, so perhaps we should indulge ourselves with something a little stronger. Do you fancy a glass of absinthe? Just one, mind you – more can be disturbing. After the first glass, you see things as you wish they were. After the second, you see them as they are not. Finally you see things as they really are, and that is the most horrible thing in the world.

Well, I'm glad I shall be able to report to posterity that you haven't lost your taste for the exotic.

Ah, now, talking of posterity, perhaps you can tell me where I stand in the estimation of the literary critics? Not that I particularly care to hear their views, but I should like to know whether they persist in confusing the artist with his subject matter and still accuse an author of immorality because it happens to be the theme of one of his books.

As a rule, no. But in your case it was rather different. For years, in England at least, they were obliged to separate you from your works to prevent the author from contaminating his books, not the other way round. It was perfectly acceptable to read your books and stage your plays, so long as your private life remained in the background. Exactly what you wanted, in other words, but for all the wrong reasons.

How perfectly wonderful! The ultimate paradox – Life imitating Art, as I always maintained it should.

Yes, but you've become quite the quotable author, your plays are performed in most civilized languages across the world, *The Picture of Dorian Gray* is now read by schoolchildren and I should say that you're almost in danger of becoming a national monument. Why, you even have a memorial window dedicated to you in Poets' Corner in Westminster Abbey.

I'm not sure I like the idea of that. It sounds a touch too conventional – though, on reflection, I suppose it's quite appropriate that I should be neither in nor out, and looking both ways at the same time.

At least you can take comfort from the fact that there are still a few dissident voices that lose no opportunity of criticizing both your art and your morality.

Excellent. I always feel that if people agree with me I must be in the wrong. Reputations, like languages, need to be on the move constantly, otherwise they grow stale. And now, dear boy, I think we should pay this nice young man who has looked after us so admirably all afternoon.

Do you have any change? I'm rather short at
the moment as the wretched hotelier where I'm
staying has threatened to impound my luggage
unless I pay him by tomorrow, and I was going to
ask you if I might borrow ...

**Really, Oscar. You ought to be able to do better
than that by now. That's the same excuse you
used twice in a month to get money from
Robbie in 1898.**

Was it? Oh dear, I'd quite forgotten that I'd
used it before – it shows the utter collapse of my
imagination. How very distressing.

**Well, I can't hold it against you. It's been such a
delightful interlude and I feel very privileged ...
I mean you've been so ... Look, here's something
to tide you over until things improve.**

So kind, so kind. Do let's meet again before too
long. I'm sure we shall.

FURTHER READING

AUTHOR'S NOTE
The text of this book draws so heavily on the works
and letters of Oscar Wilde, whether quoting directly or
by adapting his words, that to have given the sources
for every phrase would have required many pages of
endnotes. The list of books below includes all those
from which quotations used in the text have been
drawn; these are marked with an asterisk.

Quotations, direct and adapted, from *The Complete
Letters of Oscar Wilde* (copyright © Merlin Holland,
2000) are here reprinted by permission of
HarperCollins Publishers Ltd.

BOOKS
The Complete Works of Oscar Wilde, 5th edn
(Glasgow: HarperCollins, 2003)
*Karl Beckson** (ed.), *Oscar Wilde: The Critical
Heritage* (London: Routledge & Kegan Paul, 1970)
*Richard Ellmann**, *Oscar Wilde* (London: Hamish
Hamilton; New York: Knopf, 1987); read with **Horst
Schroeder**, *Additions and Corrections to Ellmann's
Oscar Wilde* (Braunschweig: privately printed, 2002)
*Frank Harris**, *Oscar Wilde* (London: Robinson; New
York: Carroll & Graf, 1997)

***Merlin Holland**, *The Wilde Album* (London: Fourth Estate, 1997; New York: Henry Holt, 1998)

***Merlin Holland**, *Irish Peacock and Scarlet Marquess* (London and New York: Fourth Estate, 2003) [published in the US as *The Real Trial of Oscar Wilde*]

***Merlin Holland & Rupert Hart-Davis** (eds.), *The Complete Letters of Oscar Wilde* (London: Fourth Estate; New York: Henry Holt, 2000)

H. Montgomery Hyde, *The Trials of Oscar Wilde* (London: Penguin Books, 1962; New York: Dover Publications, 1973)

***E.H. Mikhail** (ed.), *Oscar Wilde: Interviews and Recollections*, 2 vols. (London: Macmillan, 1979)

***Vincent O'Sullivan**, *Aspects of Wilde* (London: Constable; New York: Henry Holt, 1936)

Norman Page, *An Oscar Wilde Chronology* (London: Macmillan, 1991)

Hesketh Pearson, *The Life of Oscar Wilde* (London: Methuen; New York: Harper Bros, 1946)

***Charles Ricketts**, *Oscar Wilde: Recollections* (London: Nonesuch Press, 1932)

***Robert Harborough Sherard**, *The Life of Oscar Wilde* (London: T. Werner Laurie; New York: Dodd, Mead, 1906)

WEBSITES

The Oscar Wilde Society
www.oscarwildesociety.co.uk
The Oscholars
www.oscholars.com
CELT (Corpus of Electronic Texts, Documents of Ireland)
www.ucc.ie/celt/wilde.html